Spilt

Also by Jordan Stempleman

Cover Songs
Wallop
No, Not Today
Doubled Over
String Parade
The Travels
Facings
What's the Matter
Their Fields

Spilt

Jordan Stempleman
Winner of the Wishing Jewel Prize

Green Linden Press

GREEN LINDEN PRESS
208 Broad Street South
Grinnell, Iowa 50112
www.greenlindenpress.com

Copyright © 2025 by Jordan Stempleman
All rights reserved
Printed on recycled paper in the United States of America

Names: Stempleman, Jordan author
Title: Spilt / Jordan Stempleman.
Description: [Grinnell] : Green Linden Press, 2025.
Series: Wishing jewel series for poetic innovation ; vol. 6
Identifiers: LCCN 2025004910 | ISBN 9781961834071 paperback
Subjects: LCGFT: Poetry
Classification: LCC PS3619.T476476 S74 2025
DDC 811/.6--dc23/eng/20250220
LC record available at https://lccn.loc.gov/2025004910

Cover art: *Chief* by Adam Beris
Book design: Christopher Nelson

Green Linden Press is a nonprofit publisher dedicated to fostering excellent poetry and supporting reforestation with a portion of proceeds.

Contents

Chapter 1 *3*
Late Night Monologues *4*
Take On Me *5*
Death II *6*
No Such Elsewhere *7*
Problem-solving *8*
Passivity *9*
So Biblical *10*
Decisions *11*
Straying Young *12*
The Amateurs *13*
Negation *14*
Notices on Vibrate *15*
Masterclass *16*
Call Me *17*
Histories *18*
May I Have Your Attention, Please? *19*
The Keyholder *20*
How To Begin *21*
An Anniversary *22*
Holy Features *23*
Dustbuster *24*
Death I *25*
Less for Certain *26*
Before *27*
Unmoved *28*
Torness *29*
In Underwear, Speaking Through These Leaders *30*
The Art of Love *31*

Investigations   *32*
Hang onto It   *33*
The Two of You   *34*
Off-white Near Dark   *35*
Raw   *36*
Westport   *37*
Walk Hum   *38*
Lamplighters, Vulpes Bastille, 2022   *40*
Improper Factions   *42*
Wait Here   *46*
Gray Replaces White   *50*
Evened Instant   *51*
All Actually   *53*
At Risk of Crossing Out   *54*
A Successful Marriage   *62*
Beside the Vending Machine   *63*
Hoax Feed   *64*
The Confession   *66*
They Call It a Bargain   *67*

Note   *71*
Acknowledgments   *72*
Biography   *74*
Colophon   *75*

for V–
designer of worlds and maker of mine

Of this Spilt water, there is little to bee gathered up: it is a desperate debt.
—Ben Jonson

Groucho Marx: Tell them you're not here.
Chico Marx: Suppose they don't believe me?
Groucho Marx: They'll believe you when you start talking.
—*A Night at the Opera*

The fool who wastes his life, God rest his guts.
—Paul Westerberg

Spilt

Chapter 1

I was trucked in.
It was a rout. There
was tree shade

sometimes. Neighbors
stroking neighbors.
Walton stroking puppies.

I stray on.
I spray the yardgrass
again, stray on

until I'm up against
the ones I love.

A lot depends
so much untrue
like enemies are imitations

of perfection. My tiny
my always oncoming

home. My other nature
lived in so good.

Late Night Monologues

I once preferred pit
bulls over meadows

calmed down by odd hours
I called not gold

but dark rad
unrolling carpet.

I walk out of this bedroom
you also call a bedroom

and give it all I got.
Today I am not looking

for someone to install this plate
glass window. I am looking

for someone we can tune into
night after night after night.

Take On Me

In nights the woods
cosmos, the light

a long bead, but we write
days, think days

knowing they're the dumbest
organisms

of mattering hours.

On, leave as on. Leave
the could have could

until the undo
does the evers into ah. Testing,

testing, the starting
started now.

Death II

The slow train stroked out
and the silent animals

went pliant, and no snow
is about in the universe

but the snow around rain
before rain out.

And data, said alone, goes
better with breath—

Dash, dash, wow
that's better than wealth,

a no god long moan
of mishmash, mishmash.

Loaned atoms, loaned atoms
mishmash, mishmash.

No Such Elsewhere

Yesterday, so certain
there in the middle of it,
the clean laundry tumbling uneyed

in the age of missiles for having been born—
I look dirty one last time
before I shower today, before earth turns up time

time and time again.

The way I speak to papers
as people, as lives forever speaking
me to you—

here's where a comma goes,
here's where the choice
not so much learns as invents,

comes much later, roughly into middle age—
And everyone we've ever cared for
risks all the air

for all the remarkable love
just the same.

Problem-solving

I wanted to watch a Western,
a dirtier-the-better Western, where everybody
accidentally kills everybody
just after they say in unison
*The purpose of pop culture
is summary*, and just after they take off their hats,
and long before they ever reveal
who they really are.
Guns are allowed
if they're always going off.
And the people who do survive
survive despite all that's so reckless and slapped
together like the potential for an accident
to replace the imagination, to replace that glow
that floors us open
and pours on in.

Passivity

We are in the leftovers
of some gobbed
playboy retreat

A gully
in the universe

where the wardrobe malfunctioned
Where the meaning

was framed and the alarm
was not sounded
It personalized our experience

Make the inbox
a lot less interesting

Smile into the clown's
out-breath
until it goes right through you

Let it
go right through you
And try again when you can't
And smile again

when you can
And be there when it all does

So Biblical

the lawnmower struggled
through a birthdate of lightbulbs

chew-through of pebbles
and broccoli

and all the landscape that leans

I had a lone yellowed star
a live-in for whiteness

for slip-ups
for radical friends in heavy outline

love and rage and rhinestones
props

that I ran over
I ran over them all

Decisions

Unfinished, the bear wrestling
plays on in the other room. The afternoon
of yard work, what we call overdrive, is how to approach
a heatwave that sticks for good.
I said thanks for the free tickets
because gimme wouldn't seem funny
out in the open, a metallic temper
or someone who stares right into you
spitting cherry pits
into one paper towel after another.
The dog is at my feet
in a state of disbelief, breeding dreams
while the news, an earworm re-mangling someplace
called harmony, leaves a long tread along this unclear
border, like lakeside signage
obscured by wasp nest and buckshot. The alphabet
that gives no advice.

Straying Young

In the morning, how fast it goes, which sounds
like I care too much for the toaster.

Later, I squeeze things in so I can watch a few minutes
of drag racing on ESPN3, a pair of pantyhose

over my head, lurking around my bathroom, acting at odds
with the music, remaining on hold with my dentist

and anyone else who doesn't really care
to say more.

I sometimes remind people, talk about
your fantasies with the power drill running.

Accept that lawnmowers sound like pushed overreactions,
a whooping humming autumn to whip us

into what language we whip.
Today, I ate one hard shell taco

before completing a single-sided worksheet. I follow
so many directions:

Draw how a town behaves
just before some little storm.

The Amateurs

When I finally began disappearing, I decided
not that I was real but that I was somewhat enough.
I was in a park. The imprint in the grass
from the back of my head was there.
A child sat down in where I wasn't really
any longer, when told to sit down by her father.
He handed her a Go-GURT. We ate
Go-GURT together and slowly breathed in and out.
There was a dog, off-leash, that came up to us
and wanted what we wanted.
We resisted. And we screamed. We waited forever
for help, and help came. We returned, somewhat, to enjoying
ourselves. We sat there until it got dark
having no idea what a sunset was.

Negation

Even before the pandemic, my wife and I streamed everything together. That eighteen-season series on the way civilizations end because aliens grew bored, those cooking shows that make us feel so guilty for eating anything slightly packaged, and all those '80s sitcoms about couples soon to be zombies falling out of love. In some podcast I listened to alone on my walk to start December, I learned of the Beaker People, long gone, but whose pottery, shaped of bells and slick flesh, was plopped down unwobbled across the European landscape. And then today, while eating soup, sardines on crackers with Tabasco, I listen alone to this philosopher, someone who says negativity is really where it's at; without it, we walk back into the animal; without it, where does our happiness even begin?

Notices on Vibrate

So many affections are always at stake.
Do I stop calling some things healthcare
or include absolutely everything that lives
beside, within, amongst the living?
Do I go back to repairing whatever
works, the heart rates that equal
the coolest temperatures within these bones?
Or before I entered this room—and before
it slowly filled up and I whispered,
Have you ever seen so many bowl cuts
in one place?—know that I expected
there'd be no mayonnaise in my lap,
so much more silence because of the snow.

Masterclass

I told the good audience, this is what sex
looks like not what it feels like. The people
next door were starting up their laugh-cry
again. But let's not go there, I said to my dear
audience. Let's stay right where we are and enjoy
this togetherness, this that will never go out
of fashion.
It was now 3:30 in the afternoon. The locksmith
finally finished wrapping what was left of the furniture
in plastic, while Randy, that goofy sweetheart,
stood in the driveway in the pouring rain, ready to fuck
but not ready to make eye contact.

Call Me

I don't like talking on the phone. I once liked talking on the phone when I was young, but only when making prank calls. This was before caller ID; this was when you could open the white pages or the yellow pages to some random name or business and dial away. Once, I called a woman and told her I was lost at the mall. I was in my basement. The dog was beside me on the basement floor, licking one of his hot spots. I was probably ten or eleven, but I said, in a babyish voice, "I have to poop, and I have been here all day, and no one looks like my dad." The woman on the other line said, "I'm on my way, sweetie. Stay right next to Cinnabon, you hear me? I'm leaving now." She hung up, and I didn't laugh. I just watched the dog keep licking. I wish I could say I thought about calling her back to tell her it wasn't true, but I can't.

Once, I stood next to a man by the swings at the park and listened to him yell into his phone at his secretary while he absently pushed his baby in the toddler swing, the one that looks like a rubber diaper. His baby looked like Pat Sajak. The baby's hair was dark auburn, shiny, and looked sewn on. I think he was asleep while his father shouted, "This is what serious shit sounds like. You dropped the ball, Beth." I stared at his profile, one hand holding the phone and one absently pushing his kid. I don't want to wear black wingtips to this day. I want to find both women, say to both women, the children heard nothing that day. The children slept through it all.

Histories

The ones we loved who drowned
we called uncle. They ate black bread
in their lifetimes but never in ours.
They woke up early, ground their good
legs into brass, educated their children
in one bicycle accident after another.
Moshe had a twitch in his left eye,
the eye that was as blue as the other
stayed brown. He would ask one eye
to sing to the other. Only in bed.
Only when sketching his sheer curtains
blown haywire by the wind. His one
window facing south from Moscow.

May I Have Your Attention, Please?

For once, there's a tree over there
that looks overexerted, yellowed
in the distance, living proof
there's nothing so simple
about a summer day. But I'm a child, a light
sweater, a birthday party
in a dark bedroom.
At the magic show, she says to the audience,
I need a volunteer to come up
and look tough, pretend
to be a good listener.
Of course this is shorthand for emotion.
And the shorthand for emotion
is metaphor
and the shorthand for metaphor is emotional
distance, like the crying babysitter
saying *nevermind* over and over
to the sleeping baby.

The Keyholder

In the breakroom I handed you
a honker of paper towels and said
there is the Dust Bowl but without
the dust. The cattle, just a slice of bread
that you handed back to me
with the warm stain
of microwaved tomato soup
and a pre-recorded statement about the dangers
of mountain passes.
A stimulant worth fighting for, really.
All the while, all the while for at least
30 minutes or so, which came at no cost to Martin
or Debbie or supervisor Kyle.

How To Begin

What ends in an argument
can't be called feedback.
It's like taking a writing class
in the food court with a sea
of teenagers who break up with one another
as you grind a blank Word document
into dust.
Yesterday, I thought I'd never write again.
Today, I write again, but again
means something more
like an exaggeration
of what it felt like not to write yesterday.
Am I writing again because I used the snowblower
two mornings in a row?
Or is it because on the second morning, after the snow
blew back into my face, my neighbor
walked over and said, "That thing
sounds like it's going to bust a rod."
And afterward, I thought, expertise
has a diction the present rarely tolerates.
I begin to write—*today, I thought*—and then listen, as I imagine
one listens, eating walnuts just out of view.

An Anniversary

for V

I am filthy and careless
an old pair of scissors
left open left hidden
in one crowded drawer
after another
but you you are bravely
unprotected
like a birthday card
to the outer world
written in blossoming
snowstorm
where all the veal is left alone
for once
where fathers cry first
with a kind of love we envy
out in the open with you
and you again

Holy Features

What I like about the movies
are how all these secret assumptions
take place in our heads.
It's so chemical! I want to holler in the laundromat
to the boy struggling to shell pistachios
with his many missing teeth.
Take a stand! It's about moving away.
It's about faking the ingenious likeness of what somebody hopes
could be this quiet when their happiness
finally fits.
I hope that all my stomping around finally
makes all the difference in the world.
Because on that day I will say, mom,
forget about that dull suitcase stuffed full
of your silent audience made up of the useless and underprepared.
We are the prepared.
We are the ones who freak almost
suitable from one life to the next.

Dustbuster

I'm tired of calling things like toilet paper
a problem or the thousands of VCR tapes
never returned lost statues forgotten in forever
parked vans. Next door, a family keeps burning
anything dumb, anything vulnerable to being
held, anything that can be picked up and thrown
right in. There's the bluish thump and rising
smoke from when the old boombox hits
the reckless flames. The plastic hunk somehow
changing stations from hard rock to classical
to endless talk radio before finally calming
down. And when the ashes glow, when I somehow
discover the courage to trespass once more,
it's like peering into an obscure bite from neither
insect nor mammal. The bite simmering down
until the size of my mouth, appearing wiser
before going darker as all mouths do.

Death I

for Vic Chesnutt

Shade the lamp
and hose off the dinky. Get it on
before you think about it. While the lookouts
sit for the clinic, act easy.

One day the fish bends down
and all the air curves in, I'm told.
The sea don't know it, the grip don't know it, the runoff
don't know it, all told.

One day the damp star crosses eyes, grows staggered
for the wake-up. To take us. To reach us.

Deeps that stay for a while or for the no go.
Besides. Beside. Before now, now away.

Less for Certain

In one version of a country's history, the teacher's forehead
empties out as fog into owned open air.
But in another version, mothers are running their fingers across this
and that, the hollowed arcades from before we met
and after we eat, what we watch out for,
and what could never be enough. The cold quail.
The sparks that turn down bit by bit. Wish now
for all that can't consider, be stirred.
For all that won't consider, be stirred.
In all the strangers' faces, there's the seen
and unseen. And in all these names
that we memorize and replace, let them return to sounds
that see again. The once alien decked out in the approximate togetherness
gone alike in the wearing away.

Before

Overboard!
is a lousy pickup line

less lousy if said while sleepwalking,
while filling a frying pan
with sand.

All day long
I've been adding smells to other smells.

Some splash-down haunted
and some seem perfect for our
jib-jab, what Leon calls the yak.

Some days there's more moons
than cemeteries

more shorthand for the stuff
that dwindles long before
the neighborhoods ever do.

Unmoved

I am sitting on a stool.

I sit pooled before earlier.

I sit found for adoption

by slightness and by light.

A bulldozer snaps at the end of the day

while an hour earlier, the toilet flushes

in a barn, of all places, and flies

plus thunder plus time say something within

the words and worn.

The away shortens in the study.

And again says more about the wait

than the return.

Torness

Jellyfish love nuclear anything. Unthinking clarities, plugging up the reactor's cooling fans with their warty combs and lion manes. They'll take forever to fall for poems or fall out of love with natural history, but, in the meantime, they'll float in a slow assault into our imaginations and endless scrolling feeds. Today is Tuesday. Today, while some fish fry, the jellyfish bob closer to gasses that blister into glowwater and empty headaches. Below the surface, where science has yet to date us, the unprepared say you are mine and I am yours.

In Underwear, Speaking Through These Leaders

Whatever I lose track of
I believe will lie to me

elsewhere
give up nothing

bury itself beneath mud
whips and mutilation.

All I do
is walk around my apartment

eating bowl after bowl
of Wheat Chex

shuffling nowhere
in my dead mother's

shoulder pads.
What about the rest?

The harmless places
we sometimes trip over.

All our suddenly discovered
ways or ways out.

The Art of Love

for Kenneth Koch

You see it's only a napkin.
You see he bleached
his hair again? You see
violence is so unoriginal.
You see some stud
taking off his shoes. You see
Detroit was never a lover of
horses. You see you as a hut at
nightfall with some
film crew inside recording the
sounds of the swarming
insects outside. You see
working looks better than
work. You see something
erotic in sharing a Coca-Cola.
You see a Freemason as a
good reference. You see
whatever you can handle. You
see under
the influence and owe
everything to something so
practical. You see I'm down
for hearing things fall
but not for the falling apart.

Investigations

Unpleasant facts are what it feels like to be crowded by nothing but you. Unpleasant facts seem less about the snow cover, less about what was there before the snow came down, and everything about the melted wash merge of the thereafter. Unpleasant facts salt the imagination before drowning it. Unpleasant facts begin as glitter and end with a blowtorch. Unpleasant facts catch in the throat long before they're believed. Unpleasant facts usually steer clear of most sexual encounters, returning instead to highways, hospitals, and nations in crisis. Unpleasant facts refer to you as seagull mouth and afterimage with a bang. Unpleasant facts are not the name for unpleasant facts. Unpleasant facts don't care.

Hang onto It

It's useful when friendship drenched beautiful
steamrolls into all other living weight.
It's useful to say no wonder every substance is waiting
to finally mean lifetimes lost for lifetimes yet to come.
It's useful to begin with a near-dry memory
since we're crazy for you and refer to you so often.
It's useful to say instead air eaten mind eaten.
It's useful to view this as the companion
to all of nature: from "perhaps this is not our nature"
to "who cares" and then back.
It's useful when there's this unevenly somebody else
who blurs our voice with theirs.
It's useful to shout please forgive me
for calling this a vacation.
It's useful to write poetry when nobody's looking.
It's useful to prefer late and open with the lights on
until everything is likened enough to stand still and calm.

The Two of You

How about suspended
above a rambling hole?
How about a gradual ascent
heart-clenched and well-monitored?
How about tropical tollbooths
swapped for cathedrals?
How about cooler plans for drastic actions?
How about calling in sick to work
because of hailstones in your shoes?
How about a dream home built from all the changing rooms
you've ever locked yourself inside?
How about a boxcar full of carnivores
beside a boxcar of talent scouts?
How about divorces can only occur
underwater?
How about a freeway of alleys
with cars speeding in reverse?
How about a shoreline of perfectly fine moths?
How about compliments
that everyone agrees are true? How about opening your eyes
and seeing the light
seep through the open window
before resting your case? How about something like that?

Off-white Near Dark

It seems more like a beehive
than a movie theatre in a blackout.
It seems that you kept the telling
but somehow lost the feeling.
It seems the last time I said oral tradition
was at a Golden Corral.
It seems he has a ton of mischief in his eyes.
It seems like I've plundered
but never called it plundering.
It seems so wrong like a gong
that comes with instructions.
It seems I created some alter ego out of a bad habit.
It seems today's all bone
and tomorrow's the engravings. It seems so sad
like finding an abandoned collection of belt buckles
in an old shoebox.
It seems so easy to say that I've forgotten it or forget it or
it's not mine.

Raw

I have a sore throat.
I have a circumstance
for a freak.

There are days
when I forget your name
but never forget

once standing in front of you
in control and gone.
Look, the source is the mood,

and the mood, not knowing better,
retires before long, long
after the language.

Westport

I said yes
to going into a phone shop
but not going in.
Yes to the most dangerous
intersection and no
to executions.
And said nothing
for as long as I could
to the flat sun
long cloud sky before the sun
cutout somewhere
in that.
Could that be the end?
Could that be
the miracle method
for surface refinishing,
where the city is what it is,
a place being built
and torn apart at once?
After this cigar
my facemask smells
like uncle, while earlier,
a man my age
was cutting his toenails in his car
with the car door open
in the parking lot
of an Office Depot.
The berms make
the office building ok.
The medication on the walk back
was yum.

Walk Hum

I'm so predictable
that I begin
each song
with Adonai,
as if to deny
publicly
the Jewishness
only to try and
privately wash myself
in the comfort
of it happening
alone. So, instead,
say something
so gentile
it hurts. Like,
That's so dope,
Lucy. Such
a disappointing
success. Like
every time
I see the flag,
I know
it's happening
again.
Wow, the teeth
on this country
and the street
that says
this is not
happening this way.

The street
is not
happening
my way.
And the glove
I love
is in a nest
only for you.

Lamplighters, Vulpes Bastille, 2022

I, empurpled, think on unity
then of the frightening brilliants myriad gleam in my lamp
shadow in the mouth, a doctor's light,
a certain light, here on my desk

when I was battered by daylight
'when the light walk'
catches the dawn light
the rest is dreamed, the lamp,

only the lamps now flourish in the park,
sea, like the sun, like the sky,
is a commotion of you-know-what. It's a beautiful
possible, it simply happens, that silence we fly to

how else would eternity
on the grass in this light, shake
of divination on the move, the trace
the light grows, a white flower

morning paper—morning paper—
who said that the light of the body is the eye, and that if
we must get closer together
we've come to the place where nothing shines

a lamp too near the floor
sweetheart; or the old woman who makes a floor lamp her son;
each thing dandles
lights the whereabouts

Did I leave it, somewhere, in a margin of light?
read by the lightbulb whose paralyzed stare
vanish, merely fades into
come subito lampo   a sudden lamp in the room outside

Tonight, away begins to go
It was like the light blue handkerchief
Dawn walked on it, the sun
put the lamp on the stove

Improper Fractions

for Megan Kaminski

// if you keep stirring the darkness
the bottom will pond

will ride alone
the mist no longer elsewhere

hello sparrow crow
hello valley genus unfarmed

outstanding how the leaf hangs
above this bloom

unrolled salvation
slanting in

LEARNING WEATHER //

// a surface wail
current
and seen
in wavers

THE SCRATCH //

// pine longing but flattened
still closer

to being a driveway a window
fetched staring

wide open right through me
what's not to speak of

won't bother you
bumbled brimmed rain down

this paint
so continues not dry

NEAR YELLOW GRASS //

// brought twigs on her prom date
forgot the envelopes wore pearls

felt the best films ignore
the finish line

covered her mouth
because of Tony's breath

birds look down
on our bodies

heading home
the research shows

MY MOTHER //

Wait Here

> *To plunge into love as into a sidewalk.*
> —*Forrest Gander*

there is an audible
rhythm a density
to a person

a limitless hand
windows &
afternoons a readiness

that rides of you
defines you
by your gamble or fifty-three

levels but internally
as autonomy
the lances of friends

the goodbye the I recall
the uncured noon
want times

of sharp contrast
alert colors from
computer from eyes

or turning little job time
to commonplace smiles
& care feel

if you
didn't write good
then I

didn't write good either
& the people
with you glow

the higher glow
in meanings so clear
embroiled

& primarily but them
a quasi-porous merge
of some original

health that so melts me
as a kind of freedom
a reminder silent really

like a poem
out of conceived
partial [insert]

diastolic amnesia
of too many resonances
& we to be

as something
as we are brief
mutual & in circulation

crumpling through
the we can do
zero & blue

ridden & written off
when all mouthed
of some convenience

each morning sound
a bellwether you know
the hour of forest

crowded by dunes
faced in a good way
by inwardness

the now within the
think I shouldn't so
the language roaming

roaming as the force
of radiations
plus

refusals something
the top quark used
to refuel

the idea of
identity our earthly
makes & modes

the whiz-bang
we put forward once
the silence starts

the float of norms
of nothing now
we thin the thing

we thin the thing
so good
& so out of range

that the fires grow lost
in themselves
nothing more

than the care swept
away together
without the guide

to guide us
you hear that
right & nothing more

Gray Replaces White

When that last tree is in doubt
the love cannot scatter into recline

it's the time of tuna fish conditions
a kidney accident waiting to happen

a papaya cart that won't stop shaking
until turned over for good

and it's always the next phase that wants to know
if this time's for real
if this time's for good

to cheat while talking become quieter and easier
even quieter still

listen to the fangs tap downward against this mirror
as if to say
you are the beginning of some emptiness

always on my mind

Evened Instant

closings pause
set aside

now
for need

set aside
tension

for speed
until

the meets
emerge

and
one side

swells
of dis

and that
apart

from lovers
apart

from children
until rains

undam
until rains

unmove
until

the un
washed

come
unseen

All Actually

Real friends boss
the wind around.

A voice. An animal need.
Like if I stink

you do too.
If it's just the sunlight

again, lie down with me.
Let us say: In all that can't

consider be stirred.
In all that won't consider

be stirred.
In all the cold quail

the sparks once flowed
bit by bit.

It all depends
on how much you meant it

for how you meant it
for so much longer

than you ever knew
you could.

At Risk of Crossing Out

the advice
milkcartoned
fed

into
as the publicized
feeds—

those who loiter
within
the image

take away
from time
away

from image
I mean
try

to reheat it
return it
back to relic

the sluice
of everything
that must replace

everything:
the sale the sea
soporific

statuary
and so you say
keep doing it

you know
it
heart

the contact
soak
whatever trashes

to our words
and this old
lingering

silhouette
these extra eyes
we pop in

as the years
go on
seem

so good
at spacing
themselves

around
the strain
the tunica

of salvation—
what a gamble
what a glowing

forgotten
rhythm
to be in

the words
required
to recall

how
lovely it was
remaining

indoors
trammeled
by a sunny day

the walk
with some music:
royal navy

powder blue
grasslight
vipers

grasslight
the chorus
that manages

the emotions
from
our electronics

whatever
thought
and whatever

takes to contusion:
ice still
to glass ears

+ amnesty;
I mean
the occult

waivers
until its read
into

everything:
be able
and by

precise
less than fluent
but otherwise

nearby
like
the closest friends

after time
heard
as distances

artifacts
a long
story

returning
to the thicket
of these dreams

and largely
through news
the glass eyes

wake
cottage
the way

to total
restiveness
and order

terrible
what an audience
lists

as the preferred
encounter
standard

as plywood
standard as the wait
and the wail—

our material
that layers
it on

so thick so
devout
so prone

to snatching
until
the redesigned

go tight
or go
benign

the patter
of talk
while flame

hovers
fragrant
over the distance

left between—
tantalus
with his fruit

beyond
our theatres;
the secret

haha
to understanding
our world

these
borders
slight something

in plastic
the nameless
crack

passed by
time and time
alone

no innate range
of early
no

new news
of nicks
or a cock

cuffed
at think
or thank you

just another
phrase
that kisses

you back
into
business

or how
to unfold
or shed

that midnight
gown
of sit think

health
the halo
around

our inner
shadow
the one

that reminds
you're all the sound
the silence

gets
until
you're not

so
hats off
to this walk

to aardvarks
and understanding
blue

burgers and
oceans
and what the sky

equates
before
the big thin

A Successful Marriage

Before the arrival
there is a returning to example

a green coast
southerned calm

a sex mattress
hitting daylight
on the floor

I dance
as one mistake

after another
but you see muppet

you see the confidant
within you

no error
no warning
of we're on our own now

just the bash
and the together

the rom-com
and the breathalyzer

before
the I do

Beside the Vending Machine

The foreign country is indeed the size of you,
Tugging at the economy of your seeing, proportions .
That never break down into sameness until no, until yes

That at work I got in late because it's such an old
Fashioned place, one person sleeping while
Heavy around them, the world backed down and woke up

That while you work, you are accustomed, no god
In an unmade bed who knew not how
The emptiness about things still stands

That in this place, a reserve of the explained, it all goes
Without saying, a warehouse of everywhere,
This revolved housing, a sameness if collected only as

Seemed, as sameness to loop easily the familiar,
As foreignness itself is where we began from, and
While we are here, we will speak this circulation

Hoax Feed

crop circles
appear

overnight

ornery
rugs

that signal
the old

messages
left

as public
domain

and still

dawn's
chops

saw down
the day

roughly

before
we know

what
our looking

got us
into

The Confession

The spiritual assist
lands distant

enough
from the injury.

Goes bloom
but be not still.

The force to speak
is what drives

the near dead
at their darkest hour

to set foot in the alarms
of the just now

living.
The undisputed confession

of two naked wires
streamed

through eardrum without invoice
pouring stolen

intensities
into two survivors

who stand listening face
to face.

They Call It a Bargain

The future
has no money

but it does have
our ideas

about where the money
should go.

Try flipping off the light
right after falling

asleep in that chair.
Do you feel less

cramped
or like your tongue

has swollen
around your little

sudden heart?
What would you pay

to stay in the dark
to say

to that heart
pay anything

when you're told
cough up

the cash for feeling
this remarkably

still
still enough

to be picked up
or put down?

Note

In the poem "*Lamplighters, Vulpes Bastille, 2022*," lines are sourced from Richard Eberhart, "Light from Above"; C.K. Williams, "Light"; Anne Waldman, "Light & Shadow"; Lucian Stryk, "Light"; Gerald Stern, "Light"; Ronald Johnson, "BEAMS 21, 22, 23, The Song of Orpheus"; George Oppen, "Of Being Numerous"; Louise Glück, "The Drowned Children"; Charles Reznikoff, "Autobiography: New York"; Joshua Edwards, "The Lamp of Memory"; Hester Knibbe, "Light-Years" (translated by Jacquelyn Pope); Elizabeth Biller Chapman, "Light Thickens"; Inger Christensen, from *Light*: "If I stand" (translated by Susanna Nied); Barry Goldensohn, "Light"; Jay Wright, "Light's Interrupted Amplitude"; Frank Stanford, "The Light the Dead See"; Inger Christensen, from *Light*: "If I stand" (translated by Susanna Nied); Gail Wronsky, "Light chaff and falling leaves or a pair of feathers"; Inger Christensen, from *Light*: "It's very strange" (translated by Susanna Nied); Lynn Xu, "Earth Light: I"; Tom Clark, "A Lamp"; Russell Edson, "Let Us Consider"; John Barr, "First Light"; Johnathan Green, "One Light to Another"; Agha Shahid Ali, "Of Light"; S.P. Zitner, "Light Bulb: Lares"; Alice Jones, "Light"; Robert Blaser, "Robert Duncan"; Inger Christensen, from *Light*: "Blue Poles" (translated by Susanna Nied); Frank Stanford, "Light Blue"; James Schuyler, "Light Night"; Tom Pickard, "White Rose."

Acknowledgments

Thank you to the editors of the following publications where these poems first appeared, often in earlier versions and sometimes under different titles:

Bear Review: "May I Have Your Attention, Please?"
Bennington Review: "No Such Elsewhere"
Biscuit Hill: "An Anniversary"
Breaking the Glass: A Contemporary Jewish Poetry Anthology (GreenTower Press): "The Confession," "Less For Certain," and "Walk Hum"
Contemporary Verse 2: "Dustbuster," "MasterClass," and "Off-white Near Dark"
Curating Home: A Kansas City Poetry Anthology (Woodneath Press): "Investigations"
jubilat: "Death I"
KC Poetry Calendar: "Art of Love"
Heavy Feather Review: "All Actually," "Problem-solving," and "Unmoved"
Laurel Review: "Call Me" and "Torness"
Leveraging AI for Human-Centered Learning: A Practitioner's Guide to Culturally Responsive and Social-Emotional Classrooms (Routledge, Taylor & Francis Group): "Beside the Vending Machine," "Gray Replaces White," "Hang onto It," "How to Begin," and "Wait Here"
Lost Pilots: "Straying Young"
Matter Monthly: "Histories" "They Call It a Bargain"
TYPO: "Take on Me"
Under a Warm Green Linden: "The Amateurs" and "A Successful Marriage"

Unlearning the Hush: Oral Histories of Black Female Educators in Mississippi in the Civil Rights Era (University of Illinois Press): "Less for Certain"
Windfall Room: "Death II"

Biography

Jordan Stempleman is the author of ten books of poetry, including *Cover Songs* (The Blue Turn), *Wallop* and *No, Not Today* (Magic Helicopter Press). He also serves as the editor for *The Continental Review, Windfall Room,* and *Sprung Formal.* Since 2011, he has organized the Common Sense Reading Series in Kansas City, Missouri. In addition to his editorial work, Stempleman is an associate professor in the Liberal Arts Department and the Creative Writing Program at the Kansas City Art Institute. jordanstempleman.com

Colophon

For *Spilt*, Jordan Stempleman is the recipient of the 2025 Wishing Jewel Prize, awarded annually for a manuscript that challenges expectations of what a book of poems can be. Named for an essay in Anne Carson's *Plainwater*, the Prize champions work that questions the boundaries of genre, form, or mode while engaging the rich possibilities of lyrical expression. Other titles in this series are available from Green Linden Press:

- *schema geometrica* by Dennis Hinrichsen
- *You Would Say That* by Robin Tomens
- *Goners* by Kristi Maxwell
- *Lunette* by Bruce Bond & Walter Cochran-Bond
- *American Graphic* by JoAnne McFarland